EASY ART Quilts

AMAZING DESIGNS BASED ON TRADITION

by Christiane Meunier

CHITRA PUBLICATIONS

Your Best Value in Quilting!

First printing: 2000

Library of Congress Cataloging-in-Publication Data

Meunier, Christiane, 1952-

   Easy art quilts : amazing designs based on tradition / by Christiane Meunier.

   p. cm.

  ISBN 1-885588-34-8

  1. Patchwork--Patterns. 2. Patchwork quilts. I. Title.

  TT835 .M4857 2000

  746.46'041--dc21

                        00-040503

Edited by Debra Feece, Elsie Campbell and Virginia Jones

Design & Illustration: Kimberly Steele

Photography: VanZandbergen Photography, Brackney, Pennsylvania; Carina Woolrich, San Diego, California and Stephen J. Appel, Vestal, New York

Our Mission Statement

We publish quality quilting magazines and books that recognize, promote and inspire self-expression. We are dedicated to serving our customers with respect, kindness and efficiency.

ART Quilt

Those 2 words put next to each other are for most of us intimidating. It pushes all the "I am not good enough" and "I don't know how" buttons. Let's turn off that voice for just a little while and look at the meaning of the word 'art'. Eric Booth, in his wonderful book *The Everyday Work of Art* writes, "At the birth of the word 'art', it was a verb that meant 'to put things together'. It was not a product but a process." When we look at it this way, there is not much difference between making a quilt and making art. So what is it that makes the quilts in this book art quilts? It is their look. Just as some quilts have a country look or an antique look, some quilts have an 'art' look.

The wonderful thing about quilting is that it is such a safe medium. We never have to face the blank page or canvas! We have an endless collection of block designs and fabrics from which to choose. Let me share my process for making art quilts with you. Rarely do I deliberately choose a pattern—I usually become obsessed with one! My current obsession is the Drunkard's Path block. I see it everywhere—the moon, the sunset and in every magazine I look at. Do you have a Log Cabin, Star or Pinwheel quilt inside of you ready to be born? Even if you've used it in the last 3 quilts you've made, don't hesitate to make another one. Last year I made 8 Log Cabin quilts! I believe that quilt patterns have hidden meanings and healing powers. On a deeper level, we know which patterns correspond to what we need to express. Sometimes it takes more than 1 quilt to express what we feel. That is why a lot of artists work in series. If there is no pattern on your mind right now, just pick one!

I find it easier to choose fabric when I have an idea in mind. It can be an effect that I want to create (like in the Dalle de Verre quilt), but most of the time it is a feeling I want to express. Sometimes I play music to help me to delve deeper into my emotions. Music also seems to give me a little push to stick with my project a lit-

tle longer. Then I go through my fabric stash and intuitively pick fabrics that 'look' like I feel. I suspend all judgement when choosing fabrics. It is very powerful to see your feelings laid out in front of you in color. I realize that the emotion I'm experiencing may not feel good but it can look great in fabric. It is wonderful to tell your story without words. Each person has a unique way of seeing art. Others may see their own story in your quilt even though that story might be quite different from yours. This doesn't mean that you misinterpreted your idea in your quilt. It just means that your quilt has a broader resonance than what you intended. The fact is there is no wrong way to make an art quilt. So trust your own intuition and sense of art. Enjoy the process!

Christiane

CONTENTS

SPIRAL

You won't get lost with these simple directions!

QUILT SIZE: 69 1/2" x 75"
BLOCK SIZE: 5 1/2" square

MATERIALS

Yardage is estimated for 44" fabric.
- Assorted prints in red, purple, orange, blue and green, totaling at least 3 1/2 yards
- Assorted yellow prints, ranging from cream to dark gold, totaling at least 3/4 yard
- 1 3/8 yards mottled purple print
- 1/4 yard mottled red print
- 2 1/8 yards mottled blue print
- 4 1/4 yards backing fabric
- 74" x 79" piece of batting

CUTTING

Dimensions include a 1/4" seam allowance.
- Cut 56: 7" squares, assorted red, purple, orange, blue and green prints
- Cut 21: 6 1/8" squares, assorted red, purple, orange, blue and green prints. Then cut them in half diagonally to yield 42 large triangles. You will use 41.
- Cut 35: 4 1/4" squares, assorted red, purple, orange, blue and green prints, then cut them in half diagonally to yield 70 small triangles. You will use 69.
- Cut 69: 1 3/4" x 8 1/4" strips, assorted yellow prints
- Cut 4: 2 1/4" x 63" lengthwise strips, purple print
- Cut 7: 1" x 44" strips, red print
- Cut 4: 5" x 72" lengthwise strips, blue print
- Cut 4: 2 1/2" x 72" lengthwise strips, blue print, for the binding

PREPARATION

- Draw diagonal lines from corner to corner on the wrong side of 28 of the 7" squares.

DIRECTIONS

- Place a marked 7" square on an unmarked 7" square, right sides together. Sew 1/4" away from one diagonal line on both sides. Make 28.

- Cut the squares on the drawn lines to yield 112 pieced triangles, as shown. You will use 110. Set them aside.

- Fold a 1 3/4" x 8 1/4" yellow print strip in half crosswise. Finger press the fold to mark the center.
- Center and sew a small print triangle to one long edge of the yellow print strip, as shown.

- Center and sew a pieced triangle to the opposite edge of the yellow print strip. Trim the unit even with the edges of the small print triangle, as shown, to complete Block A. Make 69.

- Center and sew a large print triangle to a pieced triangle. Trim the unit in the same manner to complete Block B. Make 41.

ASSEMBLY

- Referring to the quilt photo lay out the blocks in 11 rows of 10.
- Stitch the blocks into rows and join the rows.
- Measure the length of the quilt. Trim 2 of the 2 1/4" x 63" purple print strips to that measurement. Sew them to the long sides of the quilt.
- Measure the width of the quilt, including the borders. Trim the remaining 2 1/4" x 63" purple print strips to that measurement. Sew them to the remaining sides of the quilt.
- Join the 1" x 44" red print strips, end to end, to make a pieced strip.
- Measure the length of the quilt. Cut two strips from the pieced strip each equal to that measurement, and sew them to the long sides of the quilt.
- Cut two strips from the remainder of the pieced strip each equal to the quilt's width, and sew them to the remaining sides of the quilt.
- Trim 2 of the 5" x 72" blue print strips to fit the quilt's length, and sew them to the long sides of the quilt.
- Trim the remaining 5" x 72" blue print strips to fit the quilt's width, and sew them to the remaining sides of the quilt.
- Finish the quilt as described in the *General Directions*, using the 2 1/2" x 72" blue print strips for the binding.

I was asked to design a quilt for the decor of Jean Houston's Mystery School. The visual theme was to be a spiral. My original quilt was 13 feet by 14 feet. *"Spiral"* (67 1/2" x 75") is a bed-sized version of that quilt. You can enter the labyrinth by one of the yellow "roads" on the left side, follow it to the center and come back out through the other one. Quilted by Joanie Keith.

Can You See What I See... Stars

Make stars from Broken Dishes!

QUILT SIZE: 41" x 45"
BLOCK SIZE: 4" square

MATERIALS

Yardage is estimated for 44" fabric.

- 1 yard batik print
- 18 fat eighths (11" x 18") hand-dyed fabrics in assorted colors
- 1 1/4 yards black for the border and binding
- 1 1/2 yards backing fabric
- 45" x 49" piece of batting

CUTTING

Dimensions include a 1/4" seam allowance.

- Cut 36: 5 3/4" squares, batik print
- Cut 2: 5 3/4" squares from each of the 18 hand-dyed fabrics
- Cut 4: 4 1/2" x 44" strips, black, for the border
- Cut 5: 2 1/2" x 44" strips, black, for the binding

NOTE: *The half-square triangles for the border will be cut after the top is completed.*

PIECING

- Draw diagonal lines from corner to corner on the wrong side of each 5 3/4" hand-dyed square. Draw horizontal and vertical lines through the centers.

For four of the 72 Broken Dishes blocks:

- Place a marked 5 3/4" hand-dyed square on a 5 3/4" batik square, right sides together. Stitch 1/4" away from the diagonal lines on both sides, as shown. Make 2 using the same hand-dyed fabric.

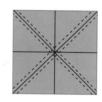

- Cut the squares on the drawn lines to yield 16 pieced squares. Press the seam allowances toward the batik.
- Lay out 4 pieced squares in 2 rows of 2, as shown. Stitch the squares into rows and join the rows to make a Broken Dishes block. Make 4.

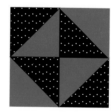

- Make 4 Broken Dishes blocks from each hand-dyed fabric for a total of 72 blocks.

ASSEMBLY

- Referring to the quilt photo, arrange the blocks in 9 rows of 8. Stitch the blocks into rows and join the rows.
- Measure the length of the quilt. Trim two 4 1/2" x 44" black strips to that measurement. Sew them to the long sides of the quilt.
- Measure the width of the quilt, including the borders. Trim the remaining 4 1/2" x 44" black strips to that measurement. Sew them to the remaining sides of the quilt.
- Decide which border blocks you want to extend into the border. Cut 2 7/8" squares from the appropriate hand-dyed fabrics, then cut them in half diagonally. Sew 2 triangles together, as shown.

- Position the pieced triangle on a border and pin it in place. Appliqué it to the border, using the tip of your needle to turn under the seam allowance. Repeat on the remaining borders, as desired.
- Finish the quilt as described in the *General Directions*, using the 2 1/2" x 44" black strips for the binding.

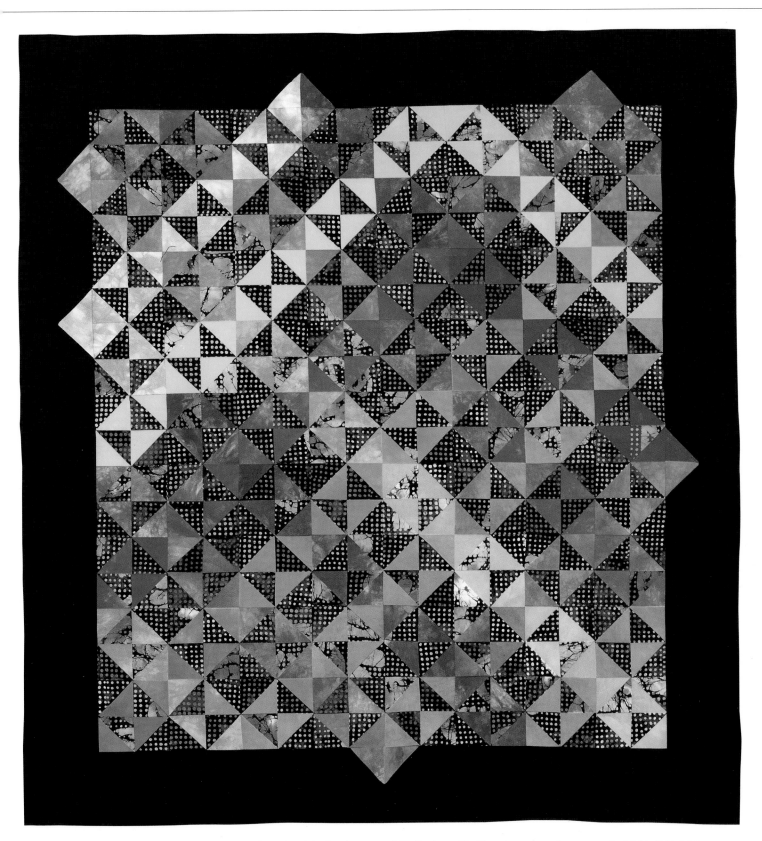

Using a traditional Broken Dishes block, Sandra M. Anderson of El Cajon, California, gave her own twist to this non-traditional looking quilt. She used batik prints and hand-dyed fabrics to give the effect of stars in **"Can You See What I See...Stars"** *(41" x 45")*.

Dalle de Verre

The black of deepest night tames the wildest of prints.

QUILT SIZE: 53 3/4" square
BLOCK SIZE: 4 1/4" square

MATERIALS

Yardage is estimated for 44" fabric.
- Assorted bright prints totaling at least 1 3/4 yards
- 2 3/4 yards black
- 3 1/2 yards backing fabric
- 58" square of batting

CUTTING

Dimensions include a 1/4" seam allowance. Cut the lengthwise black border and sashing strips before cutting smaller pieces from that fabric.
- Cut 49: 2 1/4" squares, assorted bright prints
- Cut approximately 20: 2 1/4" x 44" strips, assorted bright prints
- Cut 11: 1" x 20" strips, assorted bright prints
- Cut 4: 4 1/2" x 60" lengthwise strips, black
- Cut 2: 2 1/4" x 44 1/4" lengthwise strips, black
- Cut 8: 2 1/4" x 40 3/4" lengthwise strips, black
- Cut 3: 2 1/4" x 44" strips, black
- Cut 42: 2 1/4" x 4 3/4" strips, black
- Cut 6: 2 1/2" x 44" strips, black, for the binding

DIRECTIONS

- Place a 2 1/4" bright print square on a 2 1/4" x 44" black strip, aligning the corners. Sew the square to the strip. Place another 2 1/4" bright print square on the strip right after the first one and continue sewing. Sew a total of 17 squares to the strip in this manner.
- Repeat with the remaining 2 1/4" bright print squares and 2 1/4" x

44" black strips. Cut the units apart to yield 49 pieced units. Press the seam allowances toward the bright print squares.
- Separate the units into color families.
- Choose a 2 1/4" x 44" bright print strip to match one group of pieced units. Place a pieced unit on the 2 1/4" x 44" bright print strip, with the bright print square toward the top. Sew it to the strip. Continue sewing pieced units to the strip, as before. Start another 2 1/4"-wide bright print strip when desired or when the strip runs out. NOTE: *For more variety in your blocks, change strips often.*
- Cut the units apart and press the seam allowances toward the last strip added.
- Choose another bright print strip to match the pieced units. Place a pieced unit on the 2 1/4" x 44" bright print strip with the last strip added toward the top. Sew it to the strip. Continue sewing pieced units to the strip as before. Cut them apart and press the seam allowances toward the last strip added.
- Sew a strip to the remaining side of each pieced unit in the same manner. Cut them apart and press, as before.
- Trim a 4 3/4" square from the pieced unit, offsetting the center square as desired. Make 49.

ASSEMBLY

- Referring to the quilt photo as needed, lay out the blocks in 7 rows of 7, with 2 1/4" x 4 3/4" black strips between the blocks and 2 1/4" x 40 3/4" black strips between the rows.
- Sew the blocks and 2 1/4" x 4 3/4" strips into rows. Join the rows and 2 1/4" x 40 3/4" strips.
- Sew the remaining 2 1/4" x 40 3/4" black strips to 2 opposite sides of the quilt.
- Sew the 2 1/4" x 44 1/4" black strips to the remaining sides of the quilt.
- Sew the 1" x 20" assorted print strips together, end to end, to make a pieced strip.
- From the pieced strip, cut four 1" x 48" strips.
- Referring to the quilt photo, lay the strips along the edges of the quilt, so that the print at the end of each strip matches the print on the end of the strip it touches.
- Measure the length of the quilt. Trim the left and right side strips to that measurement. Sew them to the left and right sides of the quilt.
- Measure the width of the quilt, including the borders. Trim the remaining strips to that measurement, and sew them to the top and bottom of the quilt.
- In the same manner, trim 2 of the 4 1/2" x 60" black strips to fit the quilt's length, and sew them to opposite sides of the quilt.
- Trim the remaining 4 1/2" x 60" black strips to fit the quilt's width and sew them to the remaining sides.
- Finish the quilt as described in the *General Directions*, using the 2 1/2" x 44" black strips for the binding.

*Dalle de Verre is a contemporary form of stained glass. The term means "glass flagstone." It was introduced at the French pavilion during the New York World's Fair in 1939. Stained glass windows fascinate me. I found that large scale prints worked best to provide a feeling of transparency in **"Dalle de Verre"** (53 3/4" square). Log Cabin style blocks with large sashings create the thick concrete-like lines. Quilted by Joanie Keith.*

Broken Dishes...
and Then Some

Break from tradition using traditional fabrics and patterns.

QUILT SIZE: 44" x 40"
BLOCK SIZE: 4" square

MATERIALS

Yardage is estimated for 44" fabric.
- Assorted dark, medium and light prints totaling 2 yards
- 1/2 yard dark print for the binding
- 1 1/2 yards backing fabric
- 48" x 44" piece of batting

CUTTING

Dimensions include a 1/4" seam allowance.
- Cut 24: 4 7/8" squares, assorted prints, then cut them in half diagonally to yield 48 large triangles
- Cut 42: 2 1/2" squares, assorted prints
- Cut 94: 2 7/8" squares, assorted prints then cut them in half diagonally to yield 188 small triangles
- Cut 6: 4 1/2" squares, assorted prints
- Cut 6: 1 1/2" to 3 1/2"-wide x 44" strips assorted prints, for the borders
- Cut 1: 8" square, light print, then cut it in half diagonally to yield 2 triangles. You will use one for the border.
- Cut 1: approximately 6" x 12" rectangle, dark print, for the border corner triangle
- Cut 5: 2 1/2" x 44" strips, dark print, for the binding

DIRECTIONS

- Stitch two different print large trian-
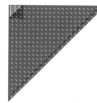
gles together along their long sides, as shown, to make a large pieced square. Make 24.

- In the same manner, stitch two different print small triangles together to make a small pieced square. Make 92. Set the remaining small triangles aside.
- Lay out four 2 1/2" print squares. Stitch them together to make a Four-Patch block, as shown. Make 8.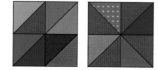
- Arrange eight 2 1/2" print squares and 92 small pieced squares in blocks of 4 units each. Stitch them into assorted blocks using any of the suggested layouts, as shown. Make 25.

ASSEMBLY

- On the design wall, lay out the 24 large pieced squares, six 4 1/2" print squares, eight Four-Patch blocks and 25 assorted blocks in 7 rows of 9. Refer to the photo for suggested placement. Stitch them into rows and join the rows.
- Sew a print border strip to the right edge of the quilt. Trim the excess even with the edges of the quilt.
- Moving counter-clockwise, sew a print border strip to the top, left side, then bottom.
- Pin the large light print triangle on the bottom border, aligning the long edge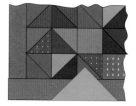
with the raw edge of the border, as shown.
- Turn under the seam allowances on the 2 short sides of the triangle and appliqué them to the border.
- Sew a print border strip to the left edge of the quilt.
- Sew a print border strip to the bottom of the quilt.
- Lay the 6" x 12" print rectangle diagonally across the top left corner of the quilt, right sides together, as shown.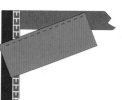
- Stitch 1/4" from the edge of the rectangle. Turn the rectangle toward the outside and check to make sure it covers the edges of the borders. Press. Trim the underneath layers 1/4" beyond the stitching line.
- Trim the corner to square the quilt.
- Referring to the quilt photo for placement suggestions, appliqué the remaining small triangles and 2 1/2" print squares randomly across the quilt and borders.
- Finish the quilt as described in the *General Directions*, using the 2 1/2" x 44" dark print strips for the binding.

Can you see the Broken Dishes blocks in this quilt? Sharyn Craig of El Cajon, California, stitched **"Broken Dishes...and Then Some"** (44" x 40") from various blocks including the Broken Dishes pattern, made from half-square triangles. The result is a stunning, vibrant wall quilt.

Little Bolshoi

Specialty fabrics enhance this asymmetrical block.

QUILT SIZE: 62" x 71"
BLOCK SIZE: 9" square

MATERIALS

Yardage is estimated for 44" fabric.

- Assorted marbled prints in earth tones, each at least 4 1/2" square
- 1/4 yard light yellow marbled print
- 1 yard dark yellow marbled print
- 1/2 yard red marbled print
- 1/2 yard each of three black marbled prints
- 2 1/2 yards black marbled print for the borders and binding
- 3 3/4 yards backing fabric
- 66" x 75" piece of batting

CUTTING

Dimensions include a 1/4" seam allowance.

- Cut 30: 4 1/2" squares, assorted earth tone marble prints
- Cut 16: 1 1/2" x 4 1/2" strips, light yellow marbled print
- Cut 16: 1 1/2" x 6 1/2" strips, light yellow marbled print
- Cut 44: 1 1/2" x 4 1/2" strips, dark yellow marbled print
- Cut 44: 1 1/2" x 6 1/2" strips, dark yellow marbled print
- Cut 6: 1 1/2" x 44" strips, dark yellow marbled print, for the middle border
- Cut 3: 3 1/2" x 44" strips, red marbled print
- Cut 1: 6 1/2" x 44" strip, each of 3 black marbled prints
- Cut 10: 3 1/2" x 6 1/2" strips, each of 3 black marbled prints
- Cut 4: 2 1/2" x 72" lengthwise strips, black marbled print, for the binding
- Cut 4: 5 1/2" x 66" lengthwise strips, black marbled print, for the outer border
- Cut 5: 2 1/2" x 44" strips, black marbled print, for the inner border

DIRECTIONS

- Sew a 3 1/2" x 44" red marbled print strip to a 6 1/2" x 44" black marbled strip, along their length, to make a pieced panel. Make 3.

- Cut ten 3 1/2" slices from each pieced panel. Set them aside.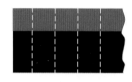

- Sew 1 1/2" x 4 1/2" light yellow marbled strips to 2 opposite sides of a 4 1/2" earth tone marbled square.

- Sew 1 1/2" x 6 1/2" light yellow marbled strips to the remaining sides of the earth tone marbled square to complete a pieced square. Make 8 using light yellow marbled strips and 22 using dark yellow marbled strips.

- Sew a 3 1/2" x 6 1/2" black marbled print strip to the left side of a pieced square, as shown.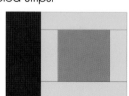

- Sew a pieced strip that contains a matching black marbled print to the top of the unit, as shown, to complete a block. Make 30.

ASSEMBLY

- Referring to the quilt photo lay out the blocks, alternating their direction, in 6 rows of 5.
- Sew the blocks into rows and join the rows.
- Join the 2 1/2" x 44" black marbled print strips, end to end, to make a pieced strip.
- Measure the length of the quilt. Cut 2 strips from the pieced strip, each equal to that measurement. Sew them to the long sides of the quilt.
- Measure the width of the quilt, including the borders. Cut 2 strips from the remainder of the pieced strip, each equal to that measurement and sew them to the remaining sides of the quilt.
- Join the 1 1/2" x 44" dark yellow marbled print strips, end to end. Cut 2 strips from the pieced strip to fit the quilt's length and sew them to the long sides of the quilt.
- Cut 2 strips from the remainder of the pieced strip to fit the quilt's width and sew them to the remaining sides of the quilt.
- Trim 2 of the 5 1/2" x 66" black marbled strips to fit the quilt's length and sew them to the long sides of the quilt.
- Trim the remaining 5 1/2" x 66" black marbled strips to fit the quilt's width and sew them to the remaining sides of the quilt.
- Finish the quilt as described in the *General Directions,* using the remaining 2 1/2" x 72" black marbled print strips for the binding.

*Last fall I attended Swan Lake performed by the Bolshoi Ballet in Moscow. When the curtains opened for the second act, I was awe-struck by the stage setting. To me it looked typically Russian—dark, deep, beautiful and soulful but very much alive. Even though the blocks in **"Little Bolshoi"** (62" x 71") are very square, they seem to dance.*

Teapots

Tea time is delightful with this cozy wallhanging.

QUILT SIZE: 43" square
BLOCK SIZE: 9" square

MATERIALS
Yardage is estimated for 44" fabric.
- 1/2 yard small (3") teapot print
- 1/2 yard large (6") teapot print
- 16 fat quarters (18" x 22") bright hand-dyed fabrics in assorted colors to coordinate with the teapot prints
- 16 hand-dyed green fabrics, each at least 4 3/4" square
- 6 fat quarters off-white prints
- 1 1/4 yards backing fabric
- 47" square of batting

CUTTING
Dimensions include a 1/4" seam allowance.
- Cut 16: 3 1/2" squares, small teapot fabric NOTE: *Carefully center a single teapot in each square*
- Cut 9: large teapots from the large teapot print, adding a 3/16" seam allowance for broderie perse appliqué
- Cut 8: 3 1/2" x 22" strips, hand-dyed fabric, for the border
- Cut 9: 2 1/2" x 22" strips, hand-dyed fabric, for the binding
- Cut 32: 3 7/8" squares, off-white prints, then cut them in half diagonally to yield 64 large triangles
- Cut 256: 2" squares, off-white prints
From each bright hand-dyed fabric:
- Cut 4: 2" squares
- Cut 8: 2" x 3 1/2" rectangles
From each hand-dyed green fabric:
- Cut 4: 2 3/8" squares, then cut them in half diagonally to yield 8 small triangles

PREPARATION
- Draw a diagonal line from corner to corner on the wrong side of each 2" off-white print square.

DIRECTIONS

For each of the sixteen blocks:
NOTE: *Use 3 different hand-dyed fabrics in each block. Select 8 small green triangles, four 2" squares and four 2" x 3 1/2" rectangles from a bright fabric, and four 2" x 3 1/2" rectangles from a second bright fabric. Use a variety of off-white prints for the background pieces in each block.*

- Lay out 2 small green triangles and one 2" bright square, as shown. Stitch them together to make a pieced triangle.
- Stitch a large off-white print triangle to the pieced triangle to make a corner square. Make 4.

- Place a marked 2" off-white print square on one corner of a 2" x 3 1/2" bright rectangle, aligning the raw edges.
- Sew on the drawn line. Trim 1/4" beyond the stitching line, as shown.
- Open the unit and press the off-white triangle toward the corner.
- Lay a marked 2" off-white print square on the opposite end of the rectangle. Sew on the drawn line.

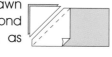

- Trim and press as before to complete a Flying Geese unit. Make 8.
- Lay out a Flying Geese unit made from the first bright fabric and a Flying Geese unit made from the second fabric. Position them with the unit made from the first bright fabric on top, as shown. Stitch them together. Make 4.

- Lay out the 4 corner squares, the 4 Flying Geese units and a 3 1/2" small teapot print square in 3 rows of 3. Sew them into rows and join the rows to complete a block. Make 16.

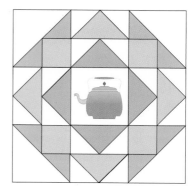

ASSEMBLY
- Lay out the blocks in 4 rows of 4. Sew the blocks into rows and join the rows.
- Referring to the quilt photo for placement, center and appliqué a large teapot in each block intersection. Use the tip of your needle to turn under the seam allowance as you stitch.
- Sew two 3 1/2" x 22" hand-dyed strips together, end to end, to make a pieced border. Make 4.
- Place a pieced border right side down on the right edge of the quilt, aligning the bottom edges and leaving the top extending past the top edge of the quilt. Pin.
- Starting approximately 3" down from the top edge of the quilt, sew the border to the quilt.
- Sew pieced borders to the bottom, left side, then top of th quilt, trimming each one even with the quilt after stitching
- Finish sewing the first border seam.
- Finish the quilt as described in the *General Directions,* using the 2 1/2" x 22" hand-dyed strips for the binding.

In a Design Challenge issued by Sharyn Craig, Margret Reap of El Cajon, California, made her interpretation of a traditional design called Delightful. She used her own hand-dyed fabrics and several very special novelty prints for **"Teapots"** (43" square).

Cosmic

You'll earn many gold stars when you stitch this design.

QUILT SIZE: 57" square
BLOCK SIZE: 4" square

MATERIALS

Yardage is estimated for 44" fabric.

- Assorted dark blue prints totaling at least 2 yards
- Assorted purple, pink, red and orange prints totaling at least 1 yard
- 1/4 yard mulitcolor print, for the pieced inner border
- 1 yard black with gold stars
- 3 1/2 yards backing fabric
- 61" square of batting

CUTTING

Dimensions include a 1/4" seam allowance.

- Cut 11: 2 1/2" x 44" strips, assorted purple, pink, red and orange prints
- Cut 20: 4 1/2" squares, assorted purple, pink, red and orange prints
- Cut 11: 2 1/2" x 44" strips, assorted dark blue prints
- Cut 140: 2 1/2" x 4 1/2" strips, assorted dark blue and black with gold stars prints
- Cut 4: 1 1/2" x 36 1/2" strips, multicolor print
- Cut 4: 1 1/2" x 36 1/2" strips, black with gold stars
- Cut 4: 2 1/2" x 36 1/2" strips, black with gold stars
- Cut 6: 2 1/2" x 44" strips, black with gold stars, for the binding

DIRECTIONS

- Stitch a 2 1/2" x 44" dark blue print strip to each 2 1/2" x 44" assorted purple, pink, red and orange print strip, along their length.

- Cut one hundred forty 2 1/2" slices from the pieced strips, as shown, to form Two-patch units.

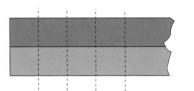

- Stitch a 2 1/2" x 4 1/2" dark blue print strip to a Two-patch unit, as shown, to complete a block. Make 115. Set the remaining Two-patch units aside to be used for the border.

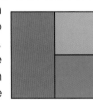

ASSEMBLY

- Referring to the quilt photo lay out 65 of the blocks, along with 16 of the 4 1/2" assorted purple, pink, red and orange print squares, in 9 rows of 9.
- Sew the blocks into rows and join the rows.
- Sew a 1 1/2" x 36 1/2" mulitcolor print strip between a 1 1/2" x 36 1/2" black with gold stars strip, and a 2 1/2" x 36 1/2" black with gold stars strip, to form a pieced border. Make 4.
- Sew pieced borders to 2 opposite sides of the quilt, placing the 2 1/2"-wide black print strip against the quilt center.
- Sew a 4 1/2" assorted purple, pink, red or orange print square to each end of the remaining pieced borders.

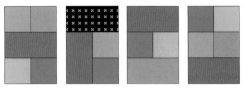

- Sew them to the remaining sides of the quilt.

For the outer pieced border:

- Sew a Two-patch unit or a 2 1/2" x 4 1/2" dark blue or black with gold stars print strip to one edge of a remaining block to make a border unit. Make 50 in any of the arrangements shown or create your own.

- Join 11 border units to make a short border. Make 2.
- In the same manner, join 14 border units to make a long border. Make 2.

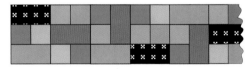

- Sew the short borders to opposite sides of the quilt.
- Sew the long borders to the remaining sides of the quilt.
- Finish the quilt as described in the *General Directions*, using the 2 1/2" x 44" black with gold stars strips for the binding.

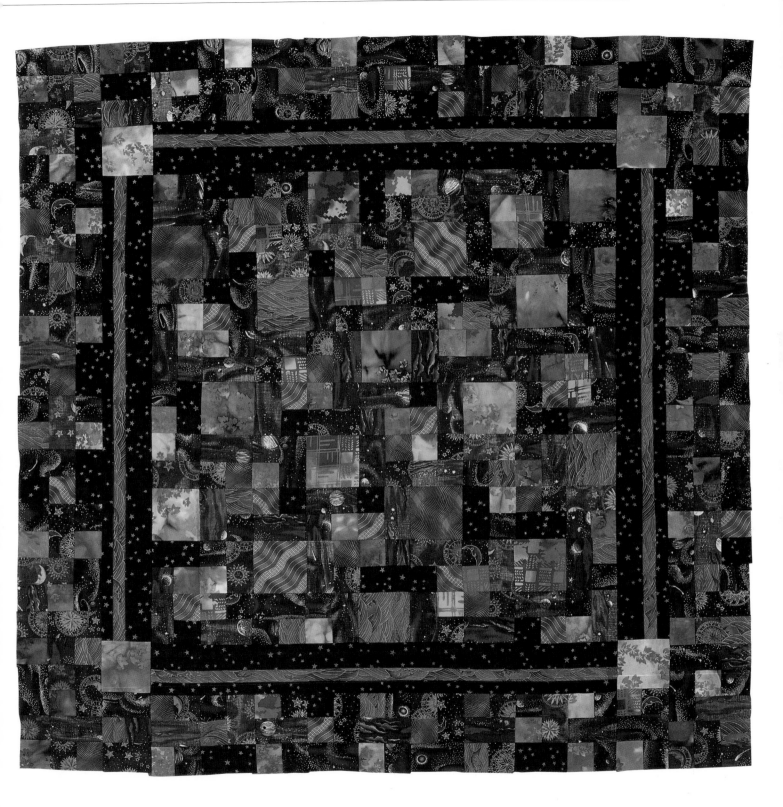

"Cosmic" *(57" square) was the first quilt I made to deal with my emotions. I was feeling depressed and angry so I chose the colors associated with those feelings - black and red. To my surprise, when finished, my quilt didn't look depressed and angry at all, but was joyful in appearance, and I found my mood changing along with my quilt.*

Lost in Space

You won't find any "black holes" in this cosmic quilt!

QUILT SIZE: 37" x 30 1/2"

MATERIALS

Yardage is estimated for 44" fabric.
- 1/2 yard blue and purple batik
- 1/4 yard red and purple batik
- Assorted navy and black cosmic prints, each at least 3 1/2" square
- 3/8 yard black with gold stars
- 3/8 yard solid black
- 1 yard backing fabric
- 41" x 35" piece of batting

CUTTING

Pattern pieces are full size and include a 1/4" seam allowance, as do all dimensions given.

- Cut 31: A, blue and purple batik
- Cut 5: A, red and purple batik
- Cut 192: B, assorted navy and black cosmic prints
- Cut 4: 2 1/4" x 36" strips, black with gold stars
- Cut 4: 2 1/2" x 44" strips, solid black, for the binding

DIRECTIONS

- Sew 2 assorted B's together to form a diamond, as shown. Make 48.
- Sew 2 more assorted B's to

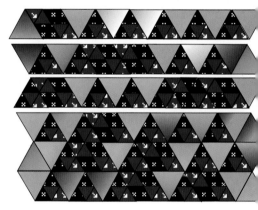

the unit to complete a Pieced Pyramid. Make 48.

ASSEMBLY

- Referring to the *Assembly Diagram*, lay out the Pieced Pyramids, and the batik A's in 6 rows.

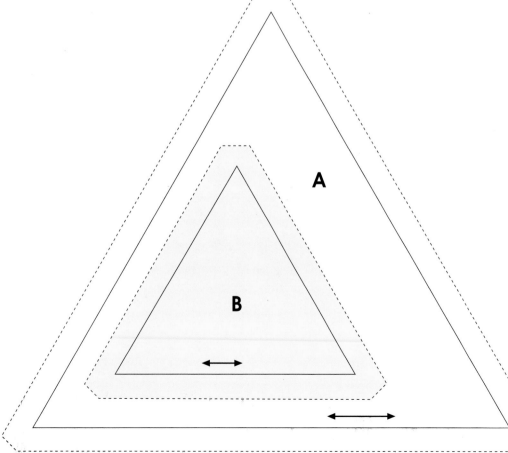

- Sew the Pieced Pyramids and batik A's into rows and join the rows.
- Trim the short sides of the quilt in a straight line, as shown, making sure to leave a 1/4" seam allowance for attaching the borders.

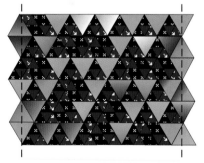

- Measure the width of the quilt. Trim 2 of the 2 1/4" x 36" black with gold stars strips to that measurement. Sew them to the top and bottom of the quilt.

A

B

*These galaxies are a visual feast of texture! By juxtaposing the soft images of batiks with a sparkling celestial print, the pyramids in **"Lost in Space"** (37" x 30 1/2") merge together as one beautiful starry night sky. I often feel like I don't belong, and bringing that emotion into existence in this quilt has made it easier for me to accept it.*

- Measure the length of the quilt, including the borders. Trim the remaining 2 1/4" x 36" black with gold stars strips to that measurement. Sew them to the sides of the quilt.

- Finish the quilt as described in the *General Directions,* using the 2 1/2" x 44" black strips for the binding.

How Did the Snails Get into My Garden!?

Coloring outside the lines reveals a secondary pattern.

QUILT SIZE: 49" x 61"
BLOCK SIZE: 4" square

MATERIALS

Yardage is estimated for 44" fabric.
- Assorted dark prints totaling at least 2 1/2 yards
- Assorted light prints totaling at least 2 1/2 yards
- 1 3/4 yards green print
- 3 yards backing fabric
- 53" x 65" piece of batting

CUTTING

Pattern pieces (on page 30) are full-size and include a 1/4" seam allowance, as do all dimensions given. NOTE: The coloration of each block is unique, therefore, the cutting list and directions refer only to the quantity and size of the pieces, not their colors. Refer to the quilt photo to choose the colors for each block, or use your own favorites. The quilter modified the templates used in some of her blocks to reduce the number of seams and varieties of fabrics used.

For each of 154 blocks:
- Cut 1: A
- Cut 2: B
- Cut 2: C

Also:
- Cut 8: 2 1/2" x 60" lengthwise strips, green print, for the borders and binding

DIRECTIONS

- Lay out the pieces for the first block as shown. Sew the 2 C's together to form a pieced triangle.
- Sew the B's to 2 sides of the A to form a second

pieced triangle, as shown.
- Sew the 2 pieced triangles together to complete a block. Make 154.

- Referring to the quilt photo lay out the blocks in 14 rows of 11. Sew the blocks into rows and join the rows.
- Measure the long sides of the quilt. Trim 2 of the 2 1/2" x 60" lengthwise green print strips to that measurement and sew them to the quilt.
- Measure the remaining sides of the quilt, including the borders. Trim 2 of the remaining 2 1/2" x 60" lengthwise green print strips to that measurement and sew them to the quilt.
- Finish the quilt as described in the *General Directions*, using the remaining 2 1/2" x 60" green print strips for the binding.

(Pattern Pieces on page 30)

ROTARY CUTTING OPTION

CUTTING

- For 2 A's, cut a 4 7/8" square, then cut it in half diagonally to yield 2 large triangles. NOTE: *They will be stitched and trimmed later to form the final diamond shape.*
- For each B, cut a 2 1/2" square.
- For 4 C's, cut a 5 1/4" square, then cut it in quarters diagonally to yield 4 medium triangles.

DIRECTIONS

- Sew 2 medium triangles (C's) together, as in the original directions, to form a pieced triangle. Set it aside.
- Draw a diagonal line from corner to corner on the wrong side of one 2 1/2" square.

- Lay the marked square on the corner of a large triangle (A), right sides together as shown, and sew on the drawn line.
- Trim 1/4" beyond the seam. Open the unit and press the seam allowance toward the darker piece.
- Lay the remaining 2 1/2" square on the same unit, right sides together, aligning it with the corner, as before. Sew 1/4" from the right edge of the square, as shown.
- Open the unit. Place it

right side down and trim the excess from the square, using the edge of the triangle as a guide.
- Turn the unit right side up and fold the trimmed square (now a triangle) back down to reveal the seam allowance. Trim the underlying triangle 1/4" beyond the seam to remove the excess fabric and complete the pieced triangle.
- Sew this pieced triangle to the C pieced triangle to complete the block. Make 154.

"How Did the Snails Get into My Garden!?" (49" x 61") is the creation of Ellie Rapp of Dana Point, California. When Sharyn Craig issued a Design Challenge to a group she calls the On-Line Quilters, Ellie began by photocopying Sharyn's original block several times. She then played with different colorations and found that she could make these simple units look like Snail's Trail blocks.

Crazy Maze Log Cabin

Feel the warmth of sunlight dancing among fallen leaves in this beauty!

QUILT SIZE: 53" square
BLOCK SIZE: 6" square

MATERIALS

Yardage is estimated for 44" fabric.
- 8 fat quarters (18" x 22") of assorted bright prints including yellow, green, dark red and blue
- 3/4 yard medium autumn leaf print
- 2 1/4 yards dark autumn leaf print
- 3 1/4 yards backing fabric
- 57" square of batting

CUTTING

Dimensions include a 1/4" seam allowance.
- Cut 64: 1 3/4" x 22" strips, assorted bright prints
- Cut 9: 1 3/4" x 44" strips, medium leaf print
- Cut 24: 1 3/4" x 44" strips, dark leaf print
- Cut 12: 2 1/2" x 44" strips, dark leaf print, for the border and binding

PIECING

For each of 36 A Blocks:

NOTE: *You will use a 1 3/4" x 22" bright print strip and approximately half of a 1 3/4" x 44" medium or dark leaf print strip for each block.*
- Cut a 1 3/4" square from a bright print strip and one from a dark leaf print strip. Place them right sides together and sew them to make a pieced unit. Press the seam allowance toward the leaf print.
- Placing the bright print square at the top, sew the unit to the dark leaf print strip, right sides together along the pieced unit's length. Cut the leaf print strip even with the pieced unit, as shown. Press the seam allowance toward the leaf print to complete round 1.

- Place the unit on a bright print strip, right sides together, so that the last fabric added is at the top. Sew them together. Cut the bright print strip even with the unit and press the seam allowance toward the bright print.

- Place the unit on the bright print strip, right sides together, so that the last fabric added is at the bottom, as shown. Sew them together. Cut and press, as before to complete round 2.

- Add bright print strips and dark leaf print strips to the unit in the same manner, to make a block with 4 rounds, as shown.
- Make 28 blocks with the dark leaf print and 8 with the medium leaf print. Label them A.

Block A

For each of 28 B Blocks:

- Reversing the position of the bright print and leaf print fabrics, make 19 blocks using the dark leaf print. Make 9 using the medium leaf print. Label them B.

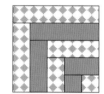

Block B

ASSEMBLY

- Lay out the 64 Half-log Cabin blocks in 8 rows of 8, referring to the quilt photo for placement ideas.
- Sew the blocks into rows and join the rows.
- Sew six 2 1/2" x 44" dark leaf print strips together, end to end, to make a long pieced strip.
- Measure the quilt. From the long pieced strip, cut 2 border strips each equal to that measurement and sew them to opposite sides of the quilt.
- Measure the width of the quilt, including the borders. From the remainder of the long pieced strip, cut 2 border strips each equal to that measurement and sew them to the remaining sides of the quilt.
- Finish the quilt as described in the *General Directions,* using the remaining 2 1/2" x 44" dark leaf print strips for the binding.

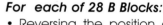

"Crazy Maze Log Cabin" *(53" square) was inspired by a drawing of the Romanesque labyrinth mosaic from the Reparatus Basilica of Orleanville, France. Quilted by Joanie Keith.*

Star Bright

Hand-dyed fabrics shimmer against a dark background.

QUILT SIZE: 44" square
BLOCK SIZE: 6" square

MATERIALS

Yardage is estimated for 44" fabric.
- 1/8 yard each of 13 hand-dyed fabrics
- 1/4 yard hand-dyed fabric, for the inner border
- 1 3/8 yards blue print
- 2 3/4 yards backing fabric
- 48" square of batting

CUTTING

Pattern pieces (on page 31) are full-size and include a 1/4" seam allowance, as do all dimension given. Cut the lengthwise blue print border and binding strips before cutting smaller pieces from that fabric.

From each of 13 hand-dyed fabrics:
- Cut 8: A; or cut four 2 7/8" squares, then cut them in half diagonally
- Cut 4: B

Also:
- Cut 4: 1 1/2" x 44" strips, hand-dyed fabric, for the inner border
- Cut 52: A, blue print; or cut twenty-six 2 7/8" squares, then cut them in half diagonally
- Cut 52: C, blue print
- Cut 20: 2 1/2" x 6 1/2" strips, blue print
- Cut 20: 2 1/2" x 4 1/2" strips, blue print
- Cut 16: 2 1/2" squares, blue print
- Cut 4: 1" x 40" strips, blue print
- Cut 9: 2 1/2" x 46" lengthwise strips, blue print, for the outer border and binding

DIRECTIONS

- Stitch a hand-dyed A to a matching hand-dyed B, as shown.

- Stitch a blue print C to the unit to complete a pieced rectangle. Make 52.

- Stitch a hand-dyed A to a blue print A, as shown, to make a pieced square. Make 52.

ASSEMBLY

- Referring to the *Assembly Diagram* lay out the pieced rectangles and pieced squares, forming stars. Fill in the spaces around the units with the 2 1/2" blue print squares and the 2 1/2" x 4 1/2" and 2 1/2" x 6 1/2" blue print strips.

- Remove the pieces from the layout for one block at a time. Join the pieces to make blocks, as shown, and return them to the layout.

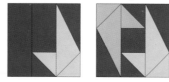

- Stitch the blocks into rows and join the rows.
- Measure the length of the quilt. Trim 2 of the 1" x 40" blue print strips to that measurement and stitch them to opposite sides of the quilt.
- Measure the width of the quilt, including the borders. Trim the remaining 1" x 40" blue print strips to that measurement and stitch them to the remaining sides of the quilt.
- In the same manner, trim 2 of the 1 1/2" x 44" hand-dyed strips to fit the quilt's length and stitch them to opposite sides of the quilt.
- Trim the remaining 1 1/2" x 44" hand-dyed strips to fit the quilt's width and stitch them to the remaining sides of the quilt.
- Trim 2 of the 2 1/2" x 46" blue print strips to fit the quilt's length and stitch them to opposite sides of the quilt.
- Trim 2 of the 2 1/2" x 46" blue print strips to fit the quilt's width and stitch them to the remaining sides of the quilt.
- Finish the quilt as described in the *General Directions,* using the remaining 2 1/2" x 46" blue print strips for the binding.

(Pattern Pieces on page 31)

Stevii Graves of San Diego, California, showcased hand-dyed fabrics in these stars which sparkle against a deep blue background. Her **"Star Bright"** (44" square) design was created by alternating the direction of the blocks and by controlling color placement.

Celebration

Spin your way into the new millennium with these galactic stars!

QUILT SIZE: 46 1/2" square
BLOCK SIZE: 3 1/4" square and
6 1/2" square

MATERIALS

Yardage is estimated for 44" fabric.
- 8 Fat quarters (18" x 22") bright batiks
- 8 Fat quarters dark blue batiks
- 1/2 yard dark blue print for the binding
- 2 3/4 yards backing fabric
- 51" square of batting

CUTTING

Pattern pieces (on page 27 and 31) are full-size and include a 1/4" seam allowance as do all dimensions given.

From the dark blue batiks:
- Cut 80: A
- Cut 64: AR
- Cut 64: C
- Cut 24: CR
- Cut 26: 3 3/4" squares
- Cut 4: E

From the bright batiks:
- Cut 80: B, in sets of 4
- Cut 64: BR, in sets of 4
- Cut 64: D, in sets of 4
- Cut 24: DR, in sets of 4
- Cut 4: F

Also:
- Cut 5: 2 1/2" x 44" strips dark blue print, for the binding

PIECING

- Sew a dark blue A to a bright B to make a blade, as shown. Make 80. Sew a dark blue AR to a bright BR.

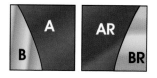

Make 64.
- Lay out 4 matching blades, as shown. Sew them together to make a large spinner block. Make 10. Make 6 reversed spinner blocks. Set the remaining blades aside for use in the border.

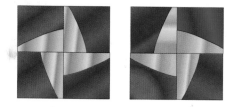

- In the same manner, stitch a dark blue print C to a bright print D to make a small blade. Make 64. Make 24 reversed blocks using the CR and DR pieces.
- Lay out 4 matching small blades, as before. Stitch them together to make a small spinner block. Make 16. Make 6 reversed small spinner blocks.
- Referring to the Assembly Diagram, lay out the 16 large spinner blocks,

fourteen 3 3/4" dark blue print squares, and 22 small spinner blocks.
- Sew the blocks into units as shown in the Assembly Diagram. Then stitch the units into horizontal rows and join the rows.
- Sew a bright F to a dark blue E, as shown, to make a corner block. Make 4.

- Lay out three 3 3/4" dark blue print squares and a corner block. Sew them together to make a corner unit, as shown. Make 4.
- Lay out two of the remaining blades, as shown. Stitch them together to make a border unit. Make 40. Make 40 reversed border units.

- Lay out 5 border units and 5 reversed border units, alternating them. Sew them together to make a border. Make 4.

- Referring to the quilt photo, sew borders to 2 opposite sides of the quilt.
- Sew a corner unit to each end of a remaining border. Make 2.

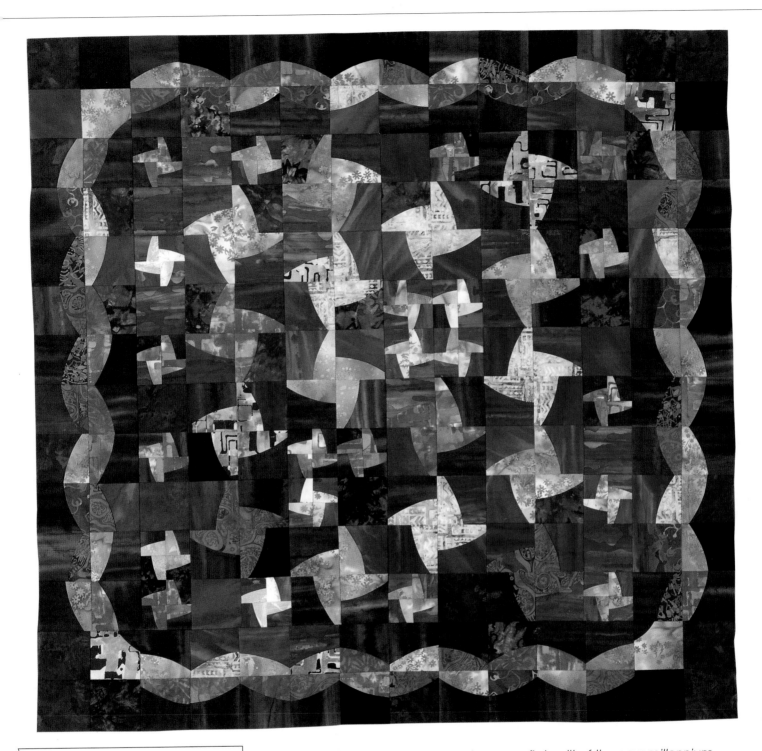

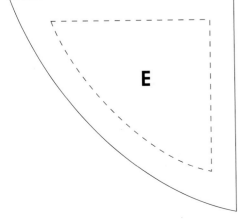

E

"Celebration" *(46 1/2" square) was my first quilt of the new millennium. Never before have we had so many opportunities. I'm very excited to be alive at such a time, and I wanted to celebrate!*

- Sew them to the remaining sides of the quilt.
- Finish the quilt as described in *General Directions,* using the 2 1/2" x 44" dark blue print strips for the binding.

(Pattern Pieces on page 31)

Enlightenment

Free-form piecing produces a one-of-a-kind design.

QUILT SIZE: 59 1/2" x 75 1/2"
BLOCK SIZE: 4" square

MATERIALS

Yardage is estimated for 44" fabric.
- Assorted batiks and hand dyed fabrics ranging from light to dark, totaling at least 4 yards
- 1 7/8 yards purple print for the inner border and binding
- 1/4 yard mottled peach print for the middle border
- 2 yards mottled blue print for the outer border
- 3 3/4 yards backing fabric
- 64" x 80" piece of batting

CUTTING

Dimensions include a 1/4" seam allowance. Cut the lengthwise purple print and mottled blue print strips, before cutting smaller pieces from those fabrics.

NOTE: *This quilt consists of 4 different blocks with centers in a variety of sizes. Make as many of each block as you wish to total 82.*

Block A   Block B

Block C   Block D

For each of 23 Block A's:
- Cut 1: square, any size between 2" and 3 1/4"
- Cut 2: 4 1/2" squares, contrasting fabric

For each of 42 Block B's:
- Cut 1: square, any size between 2" and 3"
- Cut 2: 4 1/2" squares, contrasting fabric

For each of 10 Block C's:
- Cut 1: square, any size between 2" and 3"
- Cut 4: squares, 1" or 1 1/4", contrasting fabric
- Cut 2: 4 1/2" squares, same contrasting fabric

For each of 7 Block D's:
- Cut 1: square, any size between 2" and 3 1/4"
- Cut 3: 3 1/4" x 6" strips, contrasting fabric

Also:
- Cut 83: 4 1/2" squares, assorted fabrics
- Cut 5: 2 1/2" x 62" lengthwise strips, purple print, for the binding
- Cut 4: 2 1/4" x 63" lengthwise strips, purple print, for the inner border
- Cut 6: 1" x 44" strips, mottled peach print, for the middle border
- Cut 4: 5 1/2" x 67" lengthwise strips, mottled blue print, for the outer border

DIRECTIONS

For each Block A:
- Take the pieces for one block. Cut the 4 1/2" contrasting squares in half to yield 4 rectangles.
- Center and stitch 2 rectangles to opposite sides of the print square.
- Trim the rectangles even with the edge of the center square, as shown.

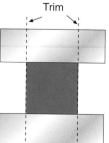

- Center and stitch the remaining rectangles to the remaining sides of the square.
- Trim the unit to 4 1/2" square, as shown, keeping the square centered. Make 23.

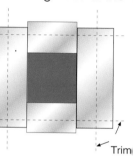

Trim

For each Block B:
- Cut the 4 1/2" contrasting squares in half diagonally to yield 4 triangles.
- Stitch 2 triangles to opposite sides of the print square. Trim the triangles even with the edges of the square, as shown.
- Center and stitch triangles to the remaining sides of the square.
- Trim the unit to 4 1/2" square, as before, keeping the on-point square centered. Make 42.

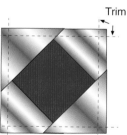

Trim

For each Block C:
- Draw a diagonal line from corner to corner on the wrong side of each 1" or 1 1/4" contrasting square.
- Lay a marked square on each of the

(Continued on page 30)

"Enlightenment" (59 1/2" x 75 1/2") was inspired by a dream which gave me the insight that giving and receiving are the in-flow and out-flow of the same energy source. One cannot exist without the other. The warm and light colors of the hand-dyed fabrics visually come forward while the other fabrics recede, creating this feeling of in-and-out flow. (From the collection of Peggy Rubin) Quilted by Joanie Keith.

4 corners of the 2" to 3" square, as shown.
- Stitch on the drawn lines. Trim 1/4" beyond the stitching lines. Press the triangles toward the corners.

- Cut the 4 1/2" contrasting print squares in half diagonally. Center and stitch triangles to 2 opposite sides of the unit.

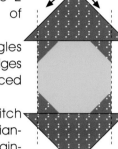

- Trim the triangles even with the edges of the center pieced unit.
- Center and stitch the remaining triangles to the remaining sides of the unit.

- Trim the unit to 4 1/2" square, as before, keeping the octagon centered. Make 10.

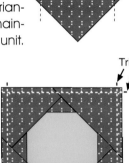

For each Block D:
- Use a ruler with a 60° angle to cut the 2 to 3 1/4" square into an equilateral triangle, as shown.

- Center and stitch a 3 1/4" x 6" contrasting strip to one side of the equilateral triangle. Press the strip away from the triangle and trim it even with the edges of the triangle, as shown.
- Stitch a 3 1/4" x 6" strip to an adjoining side of the triangle. Press it away from the triangle and trim as shown.
- Stitch a 3 1/4" x 6" contrasting strip to the remaining side of the triangle. Trim the unit to 4 1/2" square, keeping the triangle centered. Make 7.

ASSEMBLY
- Referring to the quilt photo lay out the blocks alternately with 4 1/2" squares

in 15 rows of 11. Sew the blocks and squares into rows and join the rows.
- Measure the length of the quilt. Trim 2 of the 2 1/4" x 63" purple print strips to that measurement. Sew them to the long sides of the quilt.
- Measure the width of the quilt, including the borders. Trim the remaining 2 1/4" x 63" purple print strips to that measurement. Sew them to the remaining sides of the quilt.
- Join the 1" x 44" peach strips, end to end, to make a pieced strip.
- Measure the length of the quilt. Cut 2 strips from the pieced strip each equal to that measurement and sew them to the long sides of the quilt.
- Cut 2 strips from the remainder of the pieced strip to fit the quilt's width and stitch them to the remaining sides of the quilt.
- Trim 2 of the 5 1/2" x 67" blue print strips to fit the quilt's length and stitch them to the long sides of the quilt.
- Trim the remaining 5 1/2" x 67" blue print strips to fit the quilt's width and stitch them to the remaining sides of the quilt.
- Finish the quilt as described in the *General Directions,* using the 2 1/2" x 62" purple print strips for the binding.

How Did the Snails...

Continued from page 20

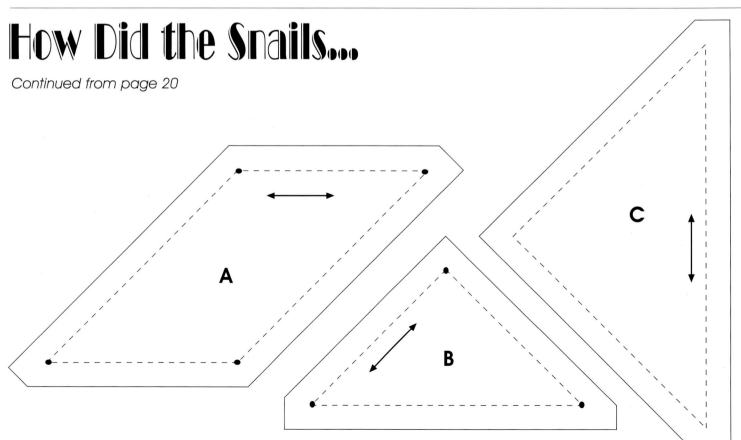

Star Bright

Continued from page 24

Celebration

Continued from page 27

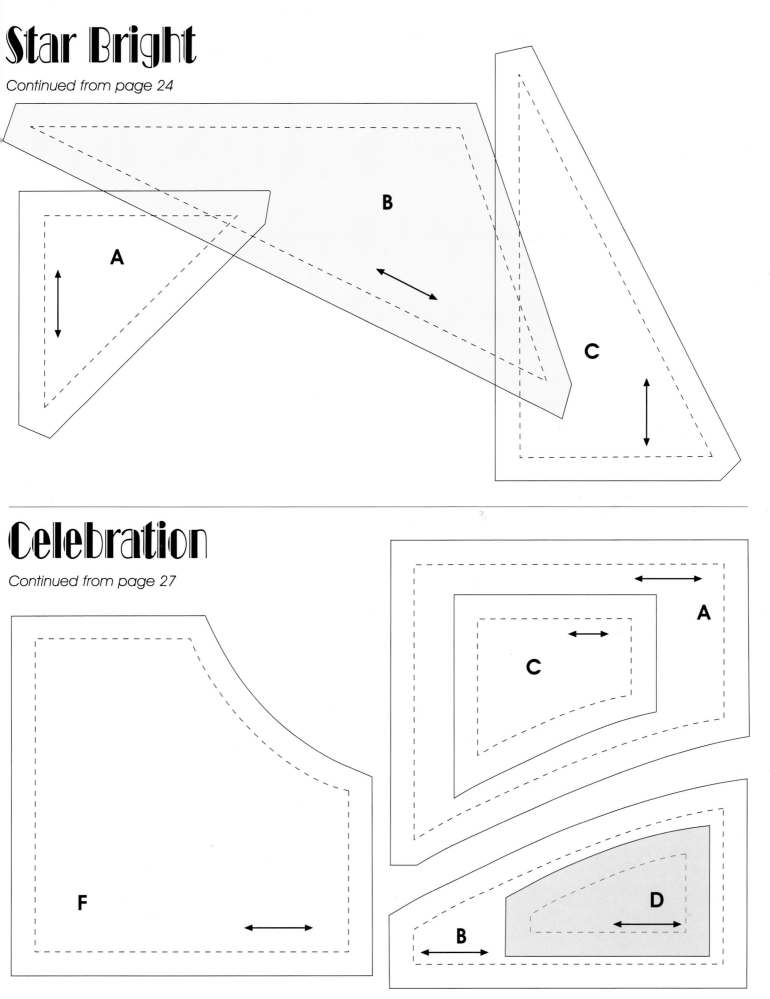

General Directions

FABRIC

Yardage requirements are based on 44" wide fabric. Listed amounts are adequate, but little is allowed for errors. I suggest using 100% cotton fabrics.

CHOOSING A PATTERN

Read through all the directions when choosing a pattern.

MACHINE SEWING

Set the stitch length to 12 stitches per inch. Cut a length of masking tape or moleskin foot pad about 1/4" x 2". Place a clear plastic ruler under and to the left of the needle aligning the right edge of he ruler 1/4" from the point of the needle along the throat plate. Stick the masking tape or moleskin in place at the ruler's edge. Feed fabric under the needle, touching this guide.

When directions call for you to start or stop stitching 1/4" from edges, backstitch to secure the seam.

TEMPLATES

Trace pattern pieces on clear plastic. Use a permanent marker to list the name of the block, total number of pieces, pattern letter and grainline on each template.

The solid line is the cutting line and the broken line is the sewing line. For machine piecing, make the template with the seam allowance. Trace around the template on the right side of the fabric. For hand piecing, make the template without the seam allowance and trace the template on the wrong side of the fabric. Add a 1/4" seam allowance as you cut the fabric piece.

PRESSING

Press with a dry iron. Press seam allowances toward the darker of the two pieces unless directed to do otherwise in the pattern. In that case, trim away 1/16" from the darker seam allowance to prevent it from showing through, if necessry.

MARKING QUILTING LINES

Mark the lines for quilting before basting the quilt together with the batting and backing. Use a very hard (#3 or #4) pencil or a chalk pencil (for darker fabrics). Many other marking tools are currently available. Test any marking method to be sure that the lines will wash out and not damage the fabric. Transfer paper quilting designs by placing fabric over the design and tracing. A light box or a brightly lit window may be necessary when using darker fabrics. Precut plastic stencils allow you to trace the quilting design onto the fabric from the front. check to be sure they fit the area you wish to quilt. Use a ruler to keep lines straight and even when marking grid lines.

Some quilting may be done without marking the top at all. Outline quilting (1/4" from the seamline) or quilting "in the ditch" can be done "by eye." Quilting "in the ditch" is done next to the seam (but not through it) on the patch opposite the pressed seam allowances.

Other straight lines may also be marked as you quilt by using the edge of masking tape as a stitching guide. For simple quilting motifs (hearts, stars, etc.) cut the shape(s) from clear, sticky-back paper (such as Contact® paper) and position them on your quilt top. These shapes can be reused many times. Do not leave masking tape or adhesive paper on your quilt top overnight. Remove it when you are finished quilting for the day to avoid leaving a residue.

BASTING

Cut the batting and backing at least 2" larger than the quilt top on all sides. Place the backing, wrong side up, on a flat surface and anchor in place with masking tape, if possible. Smooth the batting over the backing. Smooth the quilt top, right side up, over the batting. Baste the three layers together with thread or safety pins to form a quilt "sandwich." Beginning at the center of the quilt, baste horizontally first and then vertically. Add additional horizontal and vertical lines of stitches or pins approximately every 6" until the entire top is held together securely. Quilt as desired.

BINDING

After the basting is removed, trim excess batting and backing to within 1/4" of the quilt top.

For most straight-edged quilts, a double-fold French binding is an attractive, durable and easy finish. To make 1/2" finished binding, cut each strip 2 1/2" wide. Sew binding strips together with diagonal seams, trim and press seams open.

Fold the binding strip in half lengthwise, wrong side in, and press. Position the binding strip on the right side of the quilt top, aligning the raw edges of the binding with the edge of the quilt top (not so that all raw edges are even). Leave approximately 6" of binding strip free. Beginning several inches from one corner, stitch the binding to the quilt with a 1/2" seam allowance measuring from the raw edge of the backing. When you reach a corner, stop the stitching line exactly 1/2" from the edge. Backstitch, clip threads and remove the quilt from the machine. Fold the binding up and away, creating a 45° angle, as shown.

Keeping the angled folds secure, fold the binding back down. This fold should be even with the edge of the quilt top. Begin stitching at the fold.

Continue sewing the binding in this manner, stopping 6" from the starting point. To finish, fold both strips back along the edge of the quilt so that the folded edges meet about 3" from both lines of stitching and the binding lies flat on the quilt. Finger press to crease the folds. Cut both strips 1 1/4" beyond the folds.

Open both strips and place the ends at right angles to each other, right sides together. Fold the bulk of the quilt out of your way. Join the strips with a diagonal seam, as shown.

Trim the seam to 1/4" and press it open. Refold the joined strip wrong side in. Place the binding flat against the quilt and finish stitching it to the quilt. Trim the layers as needed so that the binding edge will be filled with batting when you fold the binding to the back of the quilt. Blindstitch the binding to the back of the quilt, covering the seamline.

FINISHING THE QUILT

Remove visible markings on the quilt top. Sign and date your quilt.